"Does this job pay in carrots?"

"No horsing around, Do you think Santa will like my hat?"

"Santa, I'm dreaming of a new chew toy."

"I refuse to climb into the stocking."

"I look so cute sitting beside Santa."

"Have a Meigh~~rry Christmas"

"Santa, I promise I've been a good little Guinea Pig."

"Santa's in for a surprise when he picks up his hat."

"Santa told me to watch you to see if you're naughty or nice."

"I'm ready to go sled riding."

"Merry Christmas~"

"We're guarding the fireplace for Santa."

"I heard Santa's coming to town~"

"I'm the cutest ornament on the tree~"

"I'm ready to be a Christmas card."

Merry Christmas

"I've been ripped off. This is a Charlie Brown Christmas tree."

"Where's our presents?"

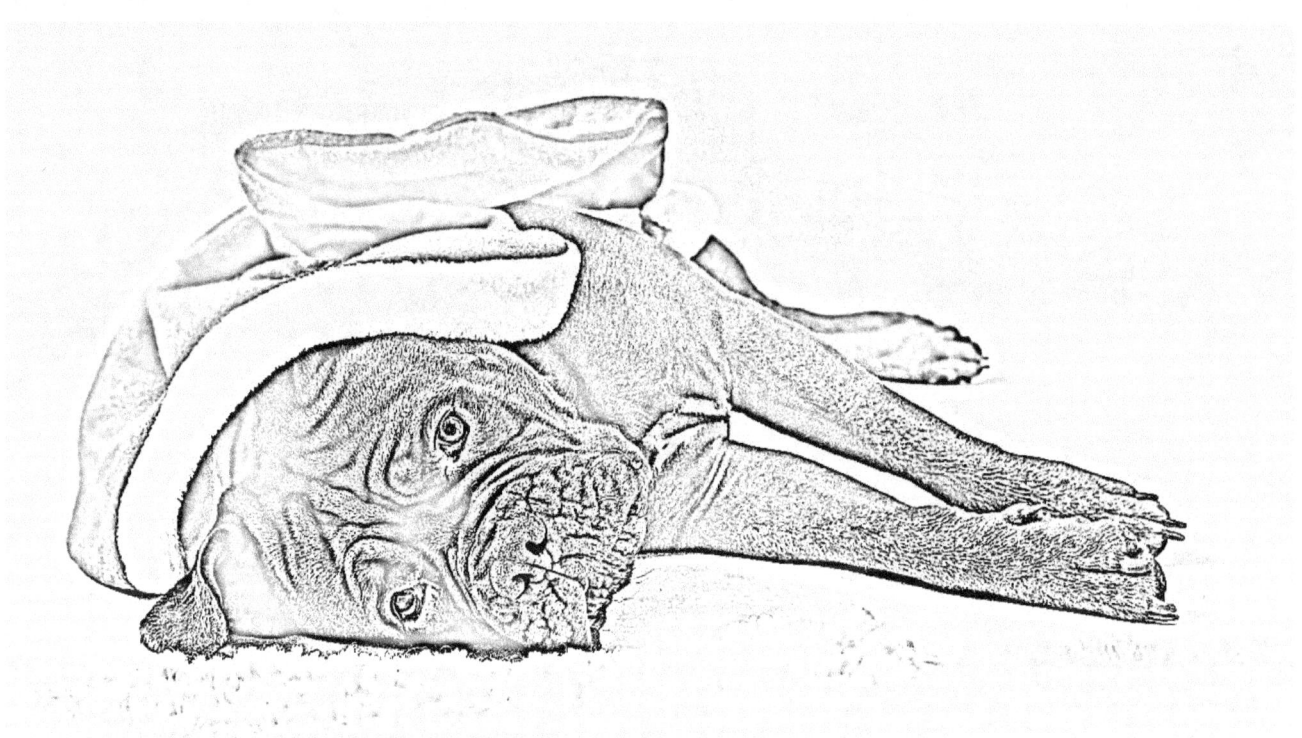

"Working for Santa is for the dogs."

"We're here to join the reindeer games."

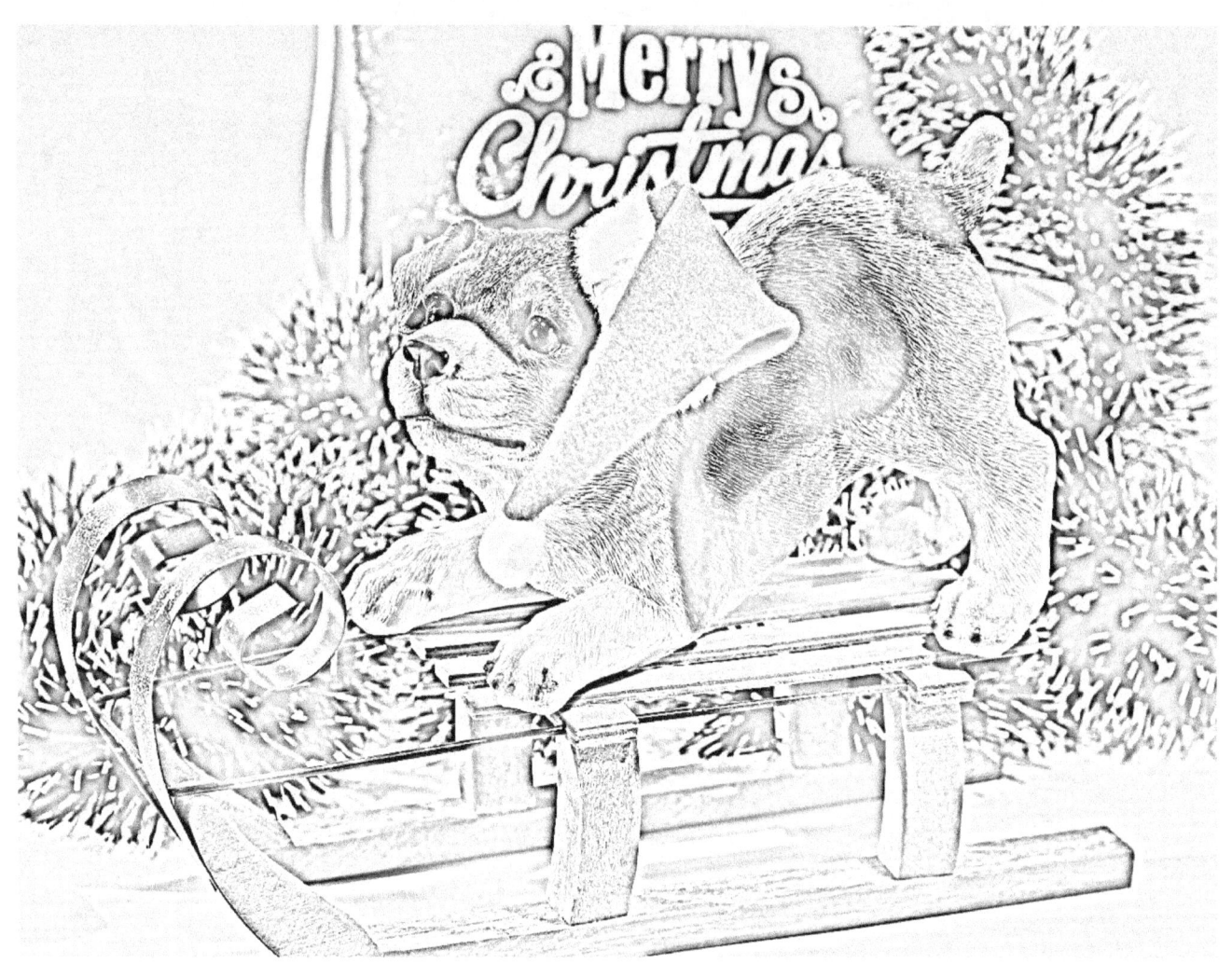

"I've got my sleigh, Where's the One-Horse?"

"I'm the best present under the tree."

"And all through the house, Not a creature was stirring... EXCEPT for this mouse."

"You thought you got presents this year? Nope~
These are mine."

"Where's my treats? I've been good this year~"

Merry Christmas!
We hope you enjoyed our book.

Watch for more coloring books by ARN Arts LLC.
http://arnarts.wixsite.com/books